SHALIM
THE
SHARK

TULSA

ISBN: 978-1-954095-34-2

Shalim the Shark

Copyright © 2021 by Adrienne C. Palma

All rights reserved.

No part of this publication may be reproduced, distributed, or transmitted in any form or by any means, including photocopying, recording, or other electronic or mechanical methods, without the prior written permission of the publisher, except in the case of brief quotations embodied in critical reviews and certain other noncommercial uses permitted by copyright law.

For permission requests, write to the publisher at the address below.

Yorkshire Publishing

1425 E 41st Pl
Tulsa, OK 74105
www.YorkshirePublishing.com
918.394.2665

Published in the USA

SHALIM ～THE～ SHARK

A Story About Sand Tiger Sharks

By
Adrienne Palma

To Michael, David, Chris, and Ann

Dream BIG

Foreword

Shalim the Shark is a wonderfully-accurate tribute to sand tiger sharks in the way it engages the reader with a pleasant, personal, character-familiarity and maintains scientific understanding of these beautiful elasmobranchs and their importance to the ocean's ecosystem. We are grateful to the author for portraying the species in such a positive light and sharing the hard work accomplished by the staff everyday at the North Carolina Aquariums to study the species, educate the public and continually find ways to make a difference in sand tiger shark conservation.

Larry R. Warner
Director
North Carolina Aquarium on Roanoke Island

Hi, my name is Shalim. I am a sand tiger shark.

Come for a swim with me as I tell you my story.

It was off the coast of North Carolina that I was born ten years ago.

As soon as I was born, just like all sand tiger sharks, I was able to swim and eat on my own.

But I stayed close to my mom for protection from bigger sharks.

When I became an adult, I was able to swim by myself.

We are slow-moving sharks. Really, what is our hurry!

The "sand" in our name is because we like the shallow water close to shore.

The "tiger" in our name is because we have big appetites!

Sand tiger sharks are grey-brown with brown spots that are unique to each shark.

We think of the spots as freckles.

I have a pointed snout and a bulky body. My mouth extends beyond my small eyes.

Did you know sand tiger sharks do not have eyelids?

I usually swim with my mouth open displaying three rows of protruding jagged-edged, sharp-pointed teeth.

I am so glad you decided to read about me. Sand tiger sharks are also known as gray nurse sharks.

Generally speaking, sharks
are feared by humans.

I get it.

Even though I may look ferocious and
menacing with my pointy teeth, I am docile.

That means sand tiger sharks are not
aggressive to humans unless threatened.

And seriously, who cannot resist my smile!

During the day, I enjoy swimming in sandy coastal waters, estuaries, shallow bays, caves, and tropical reefs at shallow depths.

I spend lots of time swimming around the shipwrecks off the Outer Banks of North Carolina.

Because we do not pose a threat toward people who swim into our domain, many scuba divers visit North Carolina's "Graveyard of the Atlantic." These humans enjoy diving in our habitat and photographing us.

What I enjoy the most is swimming in and out of the passageways of these shipwrecks lying on the ocean floor.

Like all sharks, we breathe underwater through our gills.

Sand tiger sharks are denser than water.

Did you know that sand tiger sharks
are the only sharks that come
to the surface to gulp air?

The air stays in our stomachs and
helps to keep us afloat!

That means we are buoyant. We can float
motionlessly and quietly as we watch for prey.

I am a nocturnal feeder. This means I hunt for food at night just above the ocean floor.

Due to my big appetite, an average meal can be large, and can include small fish, lobsters, squid, and crabs.

My favorite foods are bony fish, mullets, eels, and sea basses.

My sister Shiloh recently gave birth to two pups, Shep and Shadow. I'm an uncle now!

As soon as my nephews were born, they were able to eat and swim on their own just as I was able to do.

They stay close to their mother for protection from bigger sharks.

I stay close by to protect them too.

I love being an uncle!

Sand tiger sharks just have to be careful
when they are young, like my nephews now.

When we are fully grown, sand tiger sharks are
the top predators in the area where we swim.

And since we can live up to 16
years, we have lots of time to enjoy
being the king of the ocean!

Lots of sand tiger sharks live
in public aquariums.

There is one female sand tiger shark at the
North Carolina Aquarium on Roanoke Island.

She receives very good care there.

The habitat is a 285,000 gallon Graveyard of the Atlantic Habitat.

Because we have a tolerance for controlled environments, sand tiger sharks are the most widely kept large sharks in public aquariums.

The sand tiger shark loves when aquarium staff members and visitors swim with her in the habitat! Even though there are lots of other sea creatures in the habitat, like sandbar sharks and nurse sharks, the sand tiger shark enjoys the company of humans too!

Open water certified divers are allowed to dive with the sharks! Wow!

Sand tiger sharks love to have their pictures taken. There is nothing shy about us!

We love to pose for the camera!

The sand tiger shark is categorized as critically endangered on the International Union for Conservation of Nature Red List.

This identification is given to creatures that are at risk of becoming extinct.

Sand tiger sharks have protected status in the United States, Australia, and New Guinea.

I'm so glad we are protected.

critically endangered
Sand Tiger Shark

Thanks for reading my story.

You may see me sometime swimming along the coast of North Carolina.

Now, I am taking Shep and Shadow on their first adventure to swim around a shipwreck at the Graveyard of the Atlantic. (Shiloh is taking a well deserved nap.)

Fun Facts

a. The sand tiger shark (Carcharias taurus) is also known as the grey nurse shark, spotted ragged-tooth shark or blue-nurse sand tiger.

b. Sand tiger sharks can live 15 or more years.

c. Sand tiger sharks grow to a maximum length of 10.5 feet and can weigh over 400lbs.

d. Sand tiger sharks do not have bones like many other fish. Instead their skeletons are made from cartilage, which is firm but flexible connective tissue.

e. Sand tiger sharks do not have the size or teeth shape for hunting large prey.

f. Sand tiger sharks can detect electrical signals from prey about 8 to 12 inches away.

g. Sand tiger sharks have one of the lowest known reproductive rates among sharks, giving birth to only one or two large pups every two to three years.

h. Pups often spend a few months out of every year in shark nurseries. Shark nurseries are shallow, relatively secluded parts of the ocean where full-grown sharks are less common than they might be elsewhere. In 2016, researchers identified Great South Bay, a watery divide between Long Island and Fire Island, New York, as a sand tiger nursery. Other verified sand tiger nurseries are located in Plymouth and Duxbury Bays in Massachusetts.

i. Spot a Shark (https://spotashark.com/) has been conducting regular surveys of the Sand Tiger Shark population along the east coast of Australia since 2000.

j. Spot a Shark USA is a citizen science program led by the North Carolina Aquariums to engage divers in sand tiger shark research and conservation. Photos of sharks you submit to SpotASharkUSA.com help solve mysteries about these imperiled sharks.

k. Sand tiger sharks play an important ecological role on shipwrecks by controlling the variety of reef fish.

l. Sand tiger sharks are closely related to the Great White Shark and have no relationship with the Tiger Shark.

References and Resources

Sand Tiger Sharks

https://www.fisheries.noaa.gov/new-england-mid-atlantic/atlantic-highly-migratory-species/shark-identification-cooperative-shark-0
https://www.nationalgeographic.com
https://spotasharkusa.com/
https://spotashark.com/
https://kids.nationalgeographic.com/animals/fish/sand-tiger-shark/
https://oceana.org/marine-life/sharks-rays/sand-tiger-shark
https://www.coastalreview.org/2020/09/sand-tiger-sharks-call-nc-shipwrecks-home/
https://kidsanimalsfacts.com/sand-tiger-shark-facts-for-kids/

North Carolina Aquarium on Roanoke Island

http://www.ncaquariums.com/roanoke-island

Graveyard of the Atlantic

https://graveyardoftheatlantic.com/graveyard/

Graveyard of the Atlantic Museum

https://www.outerbanks.com/graveyard-of-the-atlantic.html

International Union for Conservation of Nature

https://www.iucn.org/
https://www.iucnredlist.org/species/3854/16527817

Acknowledgements

Many thanks to the following people who were my "go to" folks in writing this book. Each of you is amazing!!! I am fortunate to know you.

- Larry Warner Director, Allen McDowell, Associate Director and the hard-working staff at the North Carolina Aquarium on Roanoke Island. Everything you do is truly a labor of love!

- Barbara and John Sbunka for reading the story and offering great suggestions. The story is richer because of your input!

- Meredith Fish, Jennette's Pier, for the resources.

- David James for reading the story and offering input.

- The team at Yorkshire Publishing. You have been the BEST to work with again!

To you readers, thank you for selecting this book. The writing of this book and the upcoming books in the *Under the Sea* series is letting me live my dream everyday.

Dream BIG... then make it happen.

Other Books by Adrienne Palma

Roza Sanchez
Living the Dream
Lola the Loggerhead

Coming Soon...
the 3rd book in the *Under the Sea* series:

Dawson the Dolphin
A Story About Bottlenose Dolphins
by Adrienne Palma

www.ingramcontent.com/pod-product-compliance
Lightning Source LLC
LaVergne TN
LVHW061134181224
799426LV00023B/959